Meditations from the River

*Healing Waters
for Troubled Times*

by

CAROL ROMEO

Copyright © 2022 by Carol Romeo.

ISBN 978-1-64133-724-3 (softcover)
ISBN 978-1-64133-725-0 (ebook)

All rights reserved. No part of this book may be reproduced or transmitted in any form or by any means, electronic or mechanical, including photocopying, recording, or by any information storage and retrieval system without express written permission from the author, except in the case of brief quotations embodied in critical reviews and certain other noncommercial uses permitted by copyright law.

Printed in the United States of America.

Brilliant Books Literary
137 Forest Park Lane Thomasville
North Carolina 27360 USA

Endorsements for Meditations

Everyone's path in life is different, although at some point most of us will experience suffering. In those times, it can be difficult for us to understand our pain and God's role in our pain. In *Meditations from the River* Carol expresses her own struggle with physical illness and depression as she tries to reconcile it with the truth of God's love. I found it helpful to see that Carol's responses to a loving God became a vehicle through which she experienced a much closer relationship with Him. That relationship led her to a path of healing and growth.

Debbie
A Fellow Traveler

This book has encouraged me to keep going; it has given me a new perspective of my dark days; it has taught me to not give up in the pain but to press through to greater intimacy with Jesus. Thank you, Carol, for sharing your intimate journey. It has given me hope for a deeper relationship with Him. You inspire me to go deeper.

Sherry-Anne
Client

Carol Romeo's spiritual book, *Meditations from the River*, provides palpable hope for abiding inner peace through her heartfelt meditations and stories. She shares that God's presence on our journey through darkness and fear carries us into His enveloping and comforting love. Her own deep faith, so evident in her book, has guided my journey through intense anxiety to a healing God.

Mary Rucker
Religion Instructor

Contents

Introduction x

1. River of Compassion:
   There can be seasons of our lives when a crisis of some sort comes and punctuates our world with agony or distress. Just because we don't see a miracle does not mean that God is absent. Christ knows our pain because He took it with Him to the cross, and He sends the Holy Spirit to comfort us.

   Heavenly Dove 2
   Embracing Compassion 3
   Your Heart's a Treasure 4
   Cries in the Night 4
   My Prayer 5
   My Love 6
   How Great a Love 6
   Winter Waters 7
   Please Understand 8
   Look to the Cross 9
   He is There 10

2. Streams of His Presence:
   As we walk with Christ we have those wonderful moments when we can experience His felt presence. There are also times when heaven is silent. That is when we must lean into the Shepherd's arms and find His peace. Just as a shepherd lovingly tends his sheep and makes sure that every need is met, Christ the gentle Shepherd tends the damaged and hurt places in our souls.

   His Merciful Presence 13
   The Good Shepherd 14
   A Place by the Savior 15
   Water for My Soul 16
   Stay by Me 16
   The Promise of God 17
   Comfort in Loss 18
   The Savior's Hand 19
   A Plunge into Dark Waters 19
   Jesus, Take My Hand 20
   Present by His Spirit 21
   The Faithful One 22
   River of Peace 22
   At Peace 23

3. River of God's Goodness:
   God is a good God. However, it is difficult to remember God's goodness and faithfulness when we are in times of trial. Our pain echoes a different message into our hearts. The place to return to is the character of God. God is good. That will never change even when our circumstances change.

   His Goodness Flows to You 26
   I AM Enough 27
   Wait For the Morning 28
   The Largeness of God Can Meet My Smallness of Heart 29

Sojourners 30
A River of Hope 30
Life's Hope 31
Rivers of Refreshing and Rest 32
Rest in Me 33
Hearing the Savior's Cry 34
Come to the Cross 35

4. A Stream of Worship:
 *Worship is about God. I believe the highest form of worship is adoration of Him for **who He is**. When we can remember that, we can worship in any situation. The way we **feel** on any given day will not affect our ability to give praise to our Lord. Furthermore, He delights in our coming to Him, and He waits patiently to fill our hearts with His grace as we open to Him.*

    Worship is All About Him 38
    A New Song 39
    The Stream of His Forgiveness 40
    A Sinner's Prayer 41
    The Eyes of Our Heart 42
    Through the Eyes of My Spirit 43
    Stream of Grace 44
    Growing In Grace 44

5. River of Love:
 God's love is an extravagant love! He searched for us while we were in sin. When Jesus Christ sacrificed His life for us on the cross, He boldly demonstrated His extravagant love. The only response He waits for is our recognition of His sacrifice and our embracing of His love. As we respond, He will take us deeper and deeper into the river of His love.

    God's Deliberate Pursuit of Me 47
    The Light of His Love 48

His Bride 48
The Gift of My Love 49
A Wedding Vow 50
Deeper, Deeper Still 51
Come With Me, Child 52
Healing Waters 53
Worship the Three In One 55

6. Streams of Transformation:
   Transformation is found in the river of God. Christ desires that we be transformed into His likeness, and that seems impossible when we honestly look at ourselves. Becoming like Him would be impossible—except for His finished work on the cross on our behalf. As we yield ourselves to Him, His Spirit is able to complete the work. He becomes glorified in us.

My Night Terrors 58
Unlock the Door 59
The Lord's House 59
The Prisons of Your Soul 60
Season of Growth 61
My Heart Sings 61
A Life-changing Stream 62
Drink Ye 64
The Father Always Makes Exchanges 65
My Tattered Gift 65
The Master Craftsman 66
The Potter's Hand 67
Streams of Glory 68
The Healing Flood 69

7. Streams of Service:
   The calling on our lives—to do the same works as Jesus when He walked on this earth—begins in the heart of God. God has a purpose and a plan for your life. Moving into this plan requires a cleansing of your heart and a yielding to His will. When that transpires, your heart will be ready to receive the implant of His thoughts and dreams. What a wonder that we get to partner with Him.

Love 72
Streams of Sacrifice..72
Broken Bread, Poured Out Wine...74
A Moment's Meeting...75
A New Heart..76
Times and Seasons...77
The Master Planner..78
Serving the Cross...79
He's Alive! 80

Introduction

Meditations from the River is a collection of poems and meditations written for those of you who are experiencing distress. From my personal experience, as well as my experience as a psychotherapist, I have found that pain of all sorts tires all of our internal resources and can bring us to a place of emotional and spiritual fatigue. It is then that we must plunge into the healing river of God and experience renewal.

His river is *always* there, it is *always* flowing toward us, and it is *always* beckoning us to get in. I did not always believe that, however. Throughout the last several decades I have battled physical and emotional pain resulting from the prolonged affects of fibromyalgia. During my darkest time I imagined that Jesus had left me, and I responded by walking away from Him. Even so, His healing waters sought me out and forged a new path through the desert place to me. In the following pages you will find my prayers and cries with corresponding responses from the Lord through many different times and seasons.

There were seasons where His river flooded over me, others where the stream of His love lapped around my feet, and still others where I could hear the sound of the waters, but I could not experience them. Sometimes, in desperation, I diligently searched for His river; at other times I simply stepped in and invited the refreshing that was waiting there for me. In time, I was pleased and grateful to discover that this river and the many streams that flowed out from it contained all the grace I needed for my wearisome journey.

It is my prayer that through these pages the river of God will search you out and as you jump into it, you will find the healing, deliverance, refreshing, redemption, strength, love and comfort that you need.

I encourage you to go at your own pace as you read these meditations and drink deeply.

Open your heart to the river that is flowing to you today!

CHAPTER ONE

River of Compassion

There is a river of compassion flowing from the throne of God, which travels to us through the Holy Spirit—the One who is accurately called the Comforter. In fact, Jesus promised His followers that the Spirit would not only dwell *with* them, but also *in* them (see John 14:16–17, KJV).

Jesus promised, "I will not leave you comfortless: I will come to you" (v.18). Jesus also stated, "He who believes in Me, as the Scripture has said, out of his heart will flow rivers of living water" (John 7:38).

I became acquainted with the Holy Spirit shortly after my conversion to Christ, although my intimate relationship with Him grew over the course of my lengthy illness. He not only comforted me, but He lovingly drew me to Christ when I lacked strength and ability. Ultimately, I came to know the Spirit as the One who would usher me into the healing waters that flow from the Savior's side to me.

Fibromyalgia was my nameless enemy for a number of years before the medical profession labeled it a disease. It mercilessly ravaged my body and mind. As I battled the effects of this disease for more than twenty years, I sought the Lord and often questioned Him. I have experienced high times with Him and low times, miraculous visitations and quiet peace. There were times when His loving waters flooded my soul and other times when it trickled into the hardened places in my heart. He did not always answer me when and how I desired, but He *did* answer.

His river of compassion is always flowing, but it is up to us to open to this movement of His Spirit. Sometimes the soil of our hearts is so dry and hardened that the river of His compassion skims aimlessly over the surface, when what He desires is for us to drink deeply of His waters.

Through your cries, come to Him
    Through your doubts, move toward Him.
        Through your pain, draw close to Him.

Come to His river that is flowing to you today. Drink deeply of His love and compassion for you.

Heavenly Dove

Holy Spirit—so divine
A gift from God above.
A gift Who's freely given
To fill our hearts with love.

The Spirit comes to meet us
And free us from all fear.
He comforts our deepest pain
And dries our every tear.

Each of you who call His name
Will know the Spirit's touch.
You are children of the King;
He welcomes you as such.

> We beckon You, sweet Spirit.
> We open to Your love,
> Wonderful Holy Spirit,
> Precious Heavenly Dove.

Embracing Compassion

A sense of heaviness settled on me as I wearily slid my head back to rest against the wall. Seated in the narrow hallway adjacent to my doctor's inner office, I was irritated at this insidious disease that had terminated my vacation with my husband, Tony. We had flown home prematurely so I could receive treatment.

I closed my eyes in an attempt to numb some of the piercing pain that ran helter-skelter throughout my body and tried to dull my mind to the noise and lights around me, which amplified my discomfort.

"Soon," I told myself. "Soon I will feel better."

"Carol," I could hear the nurse call my name.

The pain sharpened with each movement as I cautiously made my way down the hall and into the treatment room. Dr. O' was waiting for me. I knew the procedure.

As he helped me onto the examining table, Dr. O' tried to make some small talk to lighten the situation. However, when he observed my demeanor, his voice softened and he took on a more reassuring role. We had done this many times. Dr. O' readied the cortisone shot needles as I unbuttoned my blouse in preparation for the procedure. Sometimes he would hit the right spots to relieve the soreness; at times he wouldn't. I was praying he would *get it* the first time. Cortisone shots were usually reserved for the worse flare-ups and this was certainly one of those times.

I really didn't mind the actual injections. My desperation at those times outweighed the treatment. Needless to say, my hope was that one day it would end. I wanted a miracle. I believed in miracles. But at this moment, God was offering me a different healing stream—the stream of His *compassion* and His sustaining power.

It is a noble act to comprehend God's promises with our minds. It is a courageous act to embrace them in our experience.

Then God said…

Your Heart's a Treasure

Your heart's a treasure
Far beyond compare.
I see and I mend
Every hurt and tear.

Embracing the pain,
The sorrow, despair
I reach out My hand
To show you My care.

I share a blessing
With you—My *most fair.*
My love transforms you
As your hurt I'll bear.

So, reach out to Me
And do not beware.
My love is faithful
You'll find I am there.

Cries in the Night

"Oh God, where are You? In this night hour Your face is hidden from me as the darkness creeps in to claim bits of my soul."

"Why can't I seem to hold fast to Your promises—the truth that You are here and that You are faithful? Your Word grows dim within my heart as waves of terror wash over me and my grip loses its connection with the warmth and stability of Your hand as time becomes my enemy."

Moments slip into hours, hours into days, days into weeks, weeks into months and months into years of pain tearing at my body and threatening my soul. My mind circles around and around:

> "How can this be happening to me?"
> "Can I gather my strength for another day, another moment?"
> "Where and when will this all cease?"
> "Is death the only answer? God forbids taking one's own life. Would I be damned to hell?"

I search within myself for some piece of solid ground to grasp onto, but I cannot find any. Pieces of my life, my very personhood, seem to be slipping away. I'm not the same person anymore. Before the pain, there was an enthusiasm in my spirit that seized each molecule of life to make it into something grand. I used to fan the flame of desire until my soul burned with the passion of the living God. It is difficult, now, to find even the scattered remains of that life I once lived.

My Prayer

> My dreams fade into tomorrow—hope dies.
> Darkness grips my hand—my spirit sighs.
> This body as a tomb in silence waits
> Till the breath of God new life creates.

> Where is Your voice amidst the maddening throng?
> Cries of pain sing their echoing song.
> Fear steals into my heart as I lay prey.
> Hear me as I come to You and pray.

My soul alone makes known the shadowed night.
Words I cannot utter of my plight
Extend beyond and beckon to Your call.
Come attend my way so I won't fall.

I slow my pace to linger at Your side.
Help me see that You will there abide.
My fingers reach to grasp Your hand in mine;
Touch my heart and let our lives entwine.

My Father said…

My Love

There is nowhere you can go that is outside the reach of My love. The encompassing darkness of the enemy cannot extinguish the flame of My love. It will continue to burn within you because My Spirit is married to the inner chambers of your heart. I will never cease to fulfill my pledge to you—the pledge of my endless love consummated by the compassionate death of My son, Jesus Christ (see John 3:16).

God, I believe. Help my unbelief.

How Great a Love

We thank You, Lord, for mercies
For tender loving care.
How seldom we recognize
You're ever present there.

For You are always watchful,
Guiding and bringing life
To those who steeped in darkness
Are in hunger and strife.

How little we know of You.
Your ways are not our own.
The kind of love that You give
So few of us have known.

Love that freely flows from You
We just cannot conceive.
Minds and hearts of fleshly men
Will not Your love receive.

Unless Your Spirit enters
And in the heart does grow—
Man can never know the love,
Which Jesus came to show.

Winter Waters

Sometimes the dark seasons of our lives seem so long. Why is the ground so cold and hard? Why are the trees barren and the brooks frozen over? Do I dare speak what I'm thinking? Is there someone to listen? Who is there in the midst of a cold dark night to listen? Parts of me feel so cold and barren I could almost shiver. I'm afraid of the night. I'm afraid that the dawn will be too far from my reach.

Will I be able to see the dawn—to feel the warmth of the sunlight—to feel hope once again? It feels so far from me right now. How can I tell You how I feel? The night has been so long. My tears have never stopped.

I keep thinking, "Surely, I will die from the heartache and the pain."

The pain comes to steal my life. It demands my attention. It strips me of my dignity. I feel so naked and alone. Why is it when it is cold and barren there seems to be no one there? There's no one to hear your whispers and to comfort your sobs.

I cry out...

God, are You there? You are so silent and still—and yet, You must be there. You have to be there. The cold and the darkness cannot keep You out. My sobs must draw You close to me. Do You hear me crying? Did You hear me today as my heart was breaking? Please don't let it break alone. Why do I feel alone when I know You must be standing at my side? Why don't You touch me so I know You are there?

Can You hear me when I cry over the pain and experience the fear that it will never end? Do You ache with me when I feel like I am losing my life—when I feel my mind slipping away from me? Do You tire of my weeping? Do You hear me when there are no words to speak? Oh God, this night is so long, so very cold and hard.

My prayer...

Please Understand

Can You hear me crying,
This child of Yours who's so afraid?
Can You hear me crying,
While by my bed I knelt and prayed?

Can You hear me crying?
I whisper now, alone, to You.
Can You hear me crying?
I hope with all my heart You do.

Can You hear me crying
Throughout a dark and lonely night?
Can You hear me crying?
I need someone to hold me tight.

Can You hear me crying
When inside my heart I struggle?
Can You hear me crying,
God, can I withstand this trouble?

Can You hear me crying
When pain cries out with all its might?
Can You hear me crying?
I want so much to see the light.

Can You hear me crying?
Please come, my Lord, and take my hand.
Can You hear me crying?
Oh please, my God, please understand.

But, God hears…

In the cold night the light-stream of the *Son* comes to warm you.

Look to the Cross

Jesus understands our pain because He carried our pain. He took your pain and mine to the cross with Him. He actually carried it in His body to the cross. On the evening before His crucifixion He began to take upon Himself our burden as He prayed, "saying, 'Father, if it is Your will, take this cup away from Me; nevertheless not My will, but Yours, be done'… And being in agony, He prayed more earnestly. Then His sweat became like great drops of blood falling down to the ground" (Luke 22:42, 44).

The medical profession tells us that blood coming out of a person's pores can happen during times of extreme agony of the soul. I do not believe that Christ was suffering for Himself and His destiny the following day. I believe He was already taking into His body the pain and anguish of each one of us. He longed for the Father to take the burden. However, this burden could only be lifted at the cross. That was the only place where sin and all the effects of sin—sickness and anguish of soul—could be eradicated.

Jesus, I thank You for carrying my pain in Your body and taking it to the cross. I leave it with You.

My prayer…

He is There

Tears fell from deep within my heart,
My grief too hard to bear.
My God, how lonely is the night,
How deep the darkness there.
How can I live another day
Amid the world's cold stare?
Happy are they and unaware—
Why doesn't someone care?

How can they know? They cannot know
The hurt that seeks to tear
At my spirit, soul and body.
Oh God, can this be fair?
As I came and knelt before Him
All my questions lay bare—
Can He know my pain? Does He care?
How can *my* grief *He* bare?

But, even as I prayed aloud,
A voice, it seemed to say,
"Why did I die at Calvary
And in the tomb I lay?
Why was I nailed upon the cross
Before the world that day—
If not to take your suffering,
To bear your hurt this way.

"You see, my love is very deep,
Much deeper than your grief
And it lifts each wounded vessel,
Each tried and broken reef.
And so, my child, when darkness comes
And seeks your heart to share,
Know by *my grace*, that I AM THERE
To comfort and to care."

Can you open your heart to the stream of compassion flowing from His cross?

CHAPTER TWO

Streams of His Presence

Nothing draws me into the river more than my pursuit of *His* presence! I became a pursuer of God the day that I first met Christ, although during the last decade my pursuit was impassioned. Christ first walked this earth so that we would know Him and His love. When He died, was resurrected, and joined His Father in the heavenly realms, He sent the third member of the Trinity (the Holy Spirit) to us on earth. It is the Holy Spirit who calls us into the river and ushers us into the depths of His glorious presence.

Oh, how I love His presence! Yes, there have been many seasons in my walk with Jesus that His presence was hidden from me. You will view some of those dark seasons in these pages, but the difficult times didn't stop me from fervently pursuing Him. I am grateful that there is a renewed emphasis among believers to seek Jesus *simply to be with Him.* I am convinced that is what He enjoys the most.

Come, seek Him and find the stream of His presence there for you today.

His Merciful Presence

I lay in silence examining the sterile surroundings of my hospital room. The chaos, which attended my life-threatening event, had subsided and all that remained was the incessant chatter of the equipment that now supported and confirmed my existence. I missed the warmth of the nurse's hand that had strengthened me throughout my ordeal, and my hand longed to be embraced once again. The bleakness of this moment was a stark contrast to the heightened care I had experienced only moments before and I reached out to grasp the hand of God.

What followed was a remarkable encounter with Him that lasted many months. It was remarkable, not just because God was present—for He is always present—but it was remarkable because His *felt presence* was so dynamic. I have often described it as dwelling inside the womb of God or in a cocoon of His protective love. Literally, a layer of His presence (three or four feet in depth) encompassed my whole body continually day and night.

In that incredible place, Jesus the *caring shepherd* revealed Himself to me. He reached out with His inviting arms, wrapped them around me, scooped me up, drew me into His secure embrace and refused to let me go (as a good shepherd would treat a wounded lamb). I had been acquainted with Jesus the Savior, but now He wanted me to know Him as the shepherd of my soul—the One who would tend my every care.

As my mind replayed the events leading up to this point I was thankful for the many evenings I had spent memorizing and meditating on the twenty-third Psalm. The words came flooding back to me in the stillness of that moment, "…Your rod and Your staff, they comfort me" (Psalm 23:4). That word "comfort" in the Hebrew language is *nacham* and is translated: "to comfort, console, extend compassion, *sigh with one who is grieving*." The *New Spirit-Filled Life Bible* adds an interesting note: "*Nacham* may have meant to breathe intensely because of deep emotion…*nacham* does not describe casual sympathy, but rather deep empathy" [1]

Contrary to some of our notions of a distant and unemotional God, the reality is that Jesus is a God who feels deeply *with* and *for* His children.

This reminds me of the time when my toddler son fell off a small step stool and broke his leg. My heart was broken over his pain, and until my husband could rush home and drive us to the hospital, all I could do was sit and rock him in my arms and pour out my *comfort* on him. There were many ways Jesus would demonstrate His comfort to me within the next several months, but for now I was content to rest my head on His shoulder and be still.

In His arms I discovered...

The Good Shepherd

I found a Lord
A Lord of mercy, tenderness, gentleness and kindness—
A Lord who comforts and consoles, who lifts me up
And surrounds me with His love,
A true and caring Shepherd.

"Thy rod and Thy staff they comfort me."
How I grew to know those words.
Jesus stood by me day and night and
Filled me with His peace.
He held my hand, He picked me up and He cared.

We all need, so much, someone to care.
Seek now the love of Jesus.
He cares for me and He cares for you.

"The Lord is my shepherd; I shall not want."

(Psalm 23:1, 4, KJV)

The Shepherd speaks…

A Place by the Savior

Oh little babe, oh child of mine,
Why won't you rest your hand in mine?
Why won't you let Me give you ease?
When in My arms your cares release.

Oh child of mine, how dear you are.
Come close to Me, stand not afar.
Come close and let Me speak your name;
You need not bow your head in shame.

Come close, My child, know My embrace;
I long to see you, face to face.
I long for you to know my love—
My presence given from above.

A heart that's filled with tender care
Is what I've come to give you there.
Please do not run away and hide;
I long to be there by your side.

Now, come to Me, my child, be blessed
When by my side, you'll find such rest.
My arms are opened wide to thee—
Come now and find your place by *Me*.

Won't you rest your head on His shoulder now and be still?

Water for My Soul

It was 1 a.m. as I stood leaning against the tile wall of my shower while the cool water soothed the welts that covered my body and mingled with the seemingly endless tears that spilled down my face.

What was it that had driven me to this point? I had an extended attack of hives that the doctors could not cure and which later became nearly fatal. I had come to the end of my own internal resources, although nobody knew that except God and me. At least I *hoped* He knew that.

Nevertheless, the brave exterior that I had put on for my family was quickly collapsing as this disease brutally attacked every part of my body. I hated it when my children saw my desperation and I could not stop the endless tirades of my mind concerning death. Part of me was afraid of dying and the other part would have welcomed the relief. I prayed, but heaven seemed distant and silent. I remained trapped in this earth-bound agonizing body.

Yet, in that shower, a part of me recognized a stream of Jesus' tears washing over me that day, running down my face, washing my soul in His tender, tender care.

All I could pray was this simple prayer…

Stay by Me

Rain in my soul
Wash the pain away.
Cleanse the wounds so deeply felt—
Wash the pain away.

Tears from my eyes
Wash the pain away.
Give me breath and give me life—
Wash the pain away.

Stay close by me
Wash the pain away.
I won't run, I'll give You time—
Wash the pain away.

Lord, here I am
Wash the pain away.
I desire to know Your love—
Wash the pain away.

Can you pray that simple prayer today?

Then God said…

The Promise of God

Child, call upon Me in the night
When sorrow dims the brightest light,
When cares wake you from your sleep,
Call on Me, your cares I'll keep.

When trouble tugs at every side
Draw close to Me and there abide.
In my heart of hearts you'll find
Solace for your troubled mind.

Bring to Me your thoughts, your worries.
I am not a God who tarries.
I will answer when you call.
You don't need to carry all.

Let Me settle and sustain you.
Give to Me the fears that drain you.
Do not keep Me from your strife,
Freely give Me of your life.

> Trust Me, child, to be beside you,
> There to care for and to guild you.
> I am there with you today.
> That is where I'll *always* stay.

Release your cares today into the stream of the One who cares. He will water your soul.

Comfort in Loss

I positioned myself in my favorite chair next to our living room window. As I quieted myself for a moment with the Lord, my attention was drawn to the large rather wonderful tree that inhabits my front yard.

"It is maybe one of the few trees in California," I thought, "whose leaves are turning colors this time of year."

It brought so much joy to my heart to see that tree and the way the early morning sun was embracing the brilliant yellow and orange leaves. I was drawn into the loveliness of it and soon recognized that a gentle peace was warming me. My thoughts shifted to my grandfather and his death about a year before and the enamoring way the Lord had met me at that time.

I was born and raised in New York and fall was my favorite season of the year, especially in upstate New York where my grandparents had lived for many years. It was this season I missed the most when my husband and I left to make our home in southern California. I don't think it was a coincidence that the Lord took my grandpa home during this heralding time of year.

The funeral took place in his hometown and his gravesite was situated on a mountainside that overlooked the blazing landscape. I was a captive audience as I stood there trying to ingest all the sights and sounds: the flowers surrounding the coffin, the guns as they were fired into the air, the pastor's consoling tones, the sight of my grandmother's grave adjacent to his and, *of course*, the vibrant splashes of yellow, red and oranges that flooded my vision and added a sweetness to my tears. My Father, who cares about me, painted the countryside for me that day.

He will paint the countryside for you.

The Savior's Hand

With His hand in mine,
He leads me along the way.
How wondrous the walk.

His strength becomes mine,
There shall be no failing now,
For He is leading.

There shall be mourning,
But He is my comforter.
There shall be sorrow,
But He is my joy.

Never to leave me,
Never to forsake me,
For He has promised.

A Plunge into Dark Waters

My husband Tony had picked me up from my hospital stay. I had imagined I would be relieved to finally go home, but I hadn't realized how protected I had felt within the confines of the hospital walls, and I felt strange sitting next to him in the car. In silence, I fixed my eyes on the rows of homes that wallpapered the street and people going about their daily tasks. I felt so far removed from everything. How would I tell Tony about the craziness I felt in my head?

As we pulled into the driveway, it dawned on me that I had not spoken to my children throughout my extended hospital stay. I became aware of my internal fragility and I started to sink. My thoughts turned to, "Why haven't I told my doctors about my emotional distress? What was I afraid of? How will I ever care for my children now?"

I tried uttering some of those thoughts to my husband, but the words would not come out. I convinced myself that time would make it better. I didn't realize that this moment would usher me into a lengthy and lonely season of darkness.

Depression—what an insidious invader it is. It can attack us at any age for any reason. What is common to all sufferers is that it seeks first to steal joy, and when its affliction is complete, it can rob us of our sense of identity (especially who we are in Christ) and it can ruin our lives.

My depression had various stages. For the most part it arrived with debilitating pain and loss of control of many areas of my life. My clinical depression lasted far too long. I should have had medical attention to treat it, but in my shame I tried desperately to hide the depth of my despair.

If you are suffering with depression, please seek help. No one should ever have to cope with it alone. There is no shame in depression. Shame is the *deception* the enemy brings.

This was my prayer. Can you make it yours?

Jesus, Take My Hand

Jesus, come and take my hand.
    Let me walk through life
        With You by my side.

As I walk over mountains and through valleys,
    Across desert places
        Where the sand is dry and untouched,
    Let me see Your footsteps
        There beside me.

Let me know the blessedness
 Of leaning fully into Your arms
  And feel the strength
 That only You can give.

In the darkness
 Cause Your light to shine.
  Make the way clear before me,
 Knowing that with every step I take
  You take one, too.

Present by His Spirit

Throughout my dark time the Lord was so gracious to me. There were precious moments when I *knew He* was at my side and His hand was available for me to hold. There were other moments, however, when my only light was His Spirit breathing life into His Word, making it mine. One such scripture was:

> Where can I go from Your Spirit? Or where can I flee from Your presence? If I ascend into heaven, You are there; if I make my bed in hell, behold, You are there. If I take the wings of the morning, and dwell in the uttermost parts of the sea, even there Your hand shall lead me, and Your right hand shall hold me.
> If I say, "Surely the darkness shall fall on me," even the night shall be light about me; indeed, *the darkness shall not hide from You,* but the night shines as the day; *the darkness and the light are both alike to You* (Psalm 139:7–12, emphasis mine).

The light of His Word shone into my darkness.

In *your* darkness, He will bring light…

The Faithful One

Do not fear where God would lead you,
Only lean and understand.
He who made the stars above you
Will not loose you from His hand.

He will ever keep you with Him,
Ever lead you by His side.
For His love is always faithful,
Ever present faithful guide.

Joy and gladness, sorrow, mourning
There our gentle Lord will be.
He is One who never leaves us;
Through the night He'll comfort thee.

Where you are, you'll surely find Him—
Through the darkness—through the night.
Jesus, He is ever faithful.
Out of darkness comes His light.

River of Peace

So many times we cry out for God's river of peace, but do we really recognize it when it comes? Jesus comforted His disciples, "Peace I leave with you, My peace I give to you; *not as the world gives do I give to you.* Let not your heart be troubled, neither let it be afraid" (John 14:27, emphasis mine). The Apostle Paul, in his letter to the Ephesians writes, "For *He Himself* is our peace" (Ephesians 2:14, emphasis mine).

As I have walked through my trials, I have discovered that I can have peace even in the midst of sorrow and grief. Note that Jesus says, "Let not your heart be troubled, neither let it be afraid." That means we must have a reason to be afraid or troubled. He doesn't promise to always take us out of our troubles, but He does promise to be with us. The psalmist David writes, "Yea, though I walk through the valley of the shadow of death, I will fear no evil; *for You are with me*; Your rod and Your staff, they *comfort* me" (Psalm 23:4, emphasis mine).

His very presence is our shelter in the storm, the rock on which we can stand. As we come to know Him better and experience His *faithfulness*, we can have peace. We may not always be able to secure that place of trust in our emotional being; nevertheless, we can begin with a spiritual decision to receive His peace as we give the Lord and ourselves the time for our emotions to catch up.

This poem was penned in the midst of my storm…

At Peace

God, set my feet
On solid ground
And work in me—
Thy grace abound.

Let me no more
A captive be.
Come cleanse me, Lord
And set me free.

To roam no more
O'er earth and sea
Alone, for in
His hands I'll be.

Protected from
The stormy gale,
Within His peace
I cannot fail.

In your storm, He wants to be your peace!

CHAPTER THREE

River of God's Goodness

Have you ever noticed how we human beings always look for *meaning* inside the circumstances we find ourselves? Sometimes that is a good thing, but not always. Some things God hides from our view until He is ready to unveil them. There are *other meanings* that we will not discover until we meet Him face to face. However, even in our lack of understanding, we can trust in the character of God.

The words on this page are insufficient to communicate the goodness and steadfastness of God. He did not meet me in the way I had imagined or longed for or even pleaded for, but He is God and He is good. And, although that knowledge did not feel quite sufficient at the time—this truth, when it gripped my heart, was enough. It was enough to carry me through the darkness to a place of greater light and strength and peace.

God's goodness is enough because it is drawn from *His* act on the cross, not mine, *His* suffering, not mine, and *His* ability to know what is right, just and fair. Life and circumstances are not always fair, but He is. Jesus is enough to bring mercy into the greatest pain, strength into the greatest defeat, and goodness into the greatest failing.

His Goodness Flows to You

In our relationship with Jesus it is crucial that we recognize His goodness *is* there with us in the middle of a dark time. In fact, my acknowledgement of that truth became the sole force that propelled me back toward God when my heart had grown disillusioned. I fail to remember the exact point at which that truth hit my heart, although I do remember that there was no other reasoning that I could bring to my experience.

I sheepishly confess that I tried everything to fix, or at the very least, to make sense of my illness.

At first, I determined that God would heal me. Therefore, I prayed all the right healing prayers, made positive faith confessions, memorized scriptural references concerning healing, read every book on healing and attended every healing service I could find. As years passed and my physical condition continued to worsen, I decided to change my stance.

Next came my martyr phase—I thought *I was completing the suffering of Christ*. Again, I consumed every book written on this subject, clung to every scripture extolling the benefits of suffering and focused on being obedient to Christ in my suffering. Ditto to my previous experience: years passed and nothing changed, except that my emotions were now breaking down and I was loosing faith. I was becoming cynical concerning my Christianity, although I kept that cleverly disguised.

Lastly, I was convinced that my trial was meant to shape my character. I fasted, repented, denied the flesh in many ways and attempted to work on the hidden attitudes of my heart. However, what remained were my words of self-recrimination and shame.

None of the above doctrinal stances are inherently incorrect. Nevertheless, my tunnel vision and strict adherence to the *rule* made it nearly impossible for me to see the *Lord* in the midst of my suffering.

Ultimately, I reached an end of my own resources…

> I stood in faith
> Until I could stand no more.
> I embraced suffering
> Until suffering embraced me.

> I bore the pain
> Until the pain consumed me.
> I hid from shame
> Until my shame *hid me*.

When I surveyed my soul I discovered:

There were no more words of faith that I could yet utter,
    no plan to destroy the work of hell,
        no act of contrition that would heal me,
            no praise that would console me.

There was no triumph,
    no grand sacrifice for Christ,
        no great transformation,
            no fulfilled joy or peace,
                  no light and no deliverance.

I inquired of God, "What will become of me? What will be the end—the grand finale—of my ordeal?"

I persisted in my search for some splendid design that God had fashioned for me in my suffering or some amazing bit of wisdom to glean from my harrowing experience, but I could find none. What would be the *something* that I could end with that would be *enough*?

I AM Enough

Then, God quietly spoke into my nothingness and said, "I am enough. My goodness is enough."

Yes, there is God! And after a lengthy deliberation I decided: God *is* good and that *is* more than enough to end with.

Do you feel like you're failing—so weak that you can't stand? There's only one truth that you need to know: *God is good and His mercy endures forever* (see Psalm 118:1). This truth is a lifeline linking you to His side.

And so, as I searched through the debris of my past and tried to bring meaning to my time of darkness, I discovered and embraced the many-faceted gem, the "goodness of God." How could I not think that He was *enough*?

He is enough for you, too. God is good—He is very good!

Wait For the Morning

I gazed at my reflected image
Tears and stains, brokenness and pain
Was all I could envision.

Where was the beauty I was destined for?
Was this God's final creation?
Certainly He held a greater plan for my life.

"I have a better plan—a plan of redemption.
It is not over yet. My resurrection life
Is at work in you.

"I conquered the grave. It didn't end there.
That was not the final work.
The greater work came in the morning."

Will you wait for the morning?
If it is evening and you are in the tomb,
Will you wait for the morning?

Will you say, "Yes, Lord, with You I can wait"?

The Largeness of God Can Meet My Smallness of Heart

I had great anticipation. I was traveling to my favorite meeting place with God—the place where He had never disappointed me—the place through which I always came away full and not wanting. Yet, I held a nagging disbelief inside. I did not identify it as a disbelief in the presence or even the power of God, but disbelief of the *intention* of God toward me about an unsettled issue between Him and me.

As I sat in the airplane glancing out the small window at the vast sky and land below, I considered the vastness of God and the greatness of His ways. The Bible defines His ways as being higher than ours (see Isaiah 55:9). Would He be disturbed that I questioned His ways yet one more time? Would He view my need to question as small or disrespectful? Nevertheless, ask I would, as I have done so many times before—just because He is a *big* God and what I was searching for was outside of my understanding.

I hope you have found, as I have through the years that God does not tire of our questions. Neither does He dismiss us because of our smallness or the smallness of our questions. What I have often found, however, is that our hearts need to make room for His answer or apparent lack of one. (That is analogous to "His ways being higher than ours"!) So, I guess the more accurate question should have been, "Was I willing to make room in my heart for His answer?" And to that query I could *honestly* reply, "I think so, I hope so, let's see…"

That week God answered my heart. All He needs from you is a "let's see…"

Sojourners

We travel on this journey—
Sojourners through this land.
Each day is numbered for us
By our Creator's hand.

He holds our lives before Him,
Small particles of sand.
He sees the distant future
That we can't understand.

So many times we wonder
And answers we demand,
Because we do not rest in
The Master's outstretched hand.

Should our vision be so small?
For when we leave this land
Crowns of glory on our heads
With Jesus we will stand.

A River of Hope

    Many circumstances throughout our lifetime can challenge our faith. There's an old saying that goes, "Trials can either make us *bitter* or *better*." Many times I recalled and rehearsed that truth during the lengthy battles I encountered in my body and emotions. Often that exercise was enough to shift my heart from a place of discontent into a position of open contemplation before God. Sadly, other seasons were marked by the stark awareness that my heart was growing cold within me.

    Psalm 42:5 reads, "Why are you cast down, O my soul? And why are you disquieted within me?" That verse produces a picture in my mind of a small child who is deeply grieved over something and for a season refuses to be comforted no matter what the caretaker does. He squirms, thrashes about and forcefully resists the loving arms that hold the power to console him. His heart is unsettled and unresponsive to the *giver*.

I find it interesting that the above verse is repeated again in Psalm 42:11 and in Psalm 43:5. I believe the psalmist was emphasizing that these conditions of our heart will occur; however, there is something we can do about it. The rest of that verse (in all three occurrences) reads, "Hope in God." It is as if the writer is reminding his own heart, "I know you feel discouraged right now, but in your distress, don't turn away from the welcoming embrace of the Father. Let Him strengthen you, soothe you and lift you up. I challenge you—have hope in God."

Do you need to challenge your heart today to hope in God? The Father's embrace will meet you there!

Life's Hope

I pray that I might see above
When nighttime shrouds Your clouds of love,
When winter falls, trees grow barren,
Oh, to trust my Rose of Sharon.

Darkness can never cancel light.
Spring must follow the winter's night.
Trees must blossom and rain must fall,
They're conscious of my Savior's call.

Yesterdays become tomorrow.
Comfort sooths a heart of sorrow.
Sad memory replaces pain,
Which once the heart held in disdain.

Brokenness turns into gladness,
Happiness in place of sadness,
Waves of love sent to cleanse the fear
And wash away our every tear.

> Beloved, I pray, be not afraid
> When winter beckons to invade.
> Be aware that in God's timing
> Resurrection follows dying.

Rivers of Refreshing and Rest

Rest. It seems like such an easy command from our Lord, and yet I find that it is one of the more difficult to follow. Why is that? There are countless reasons, but one of the most prominent is our inability to minimize our own actions and let God act. God's Word declares, "Be still, and know that I *am* God" (Psalm 46:10). **I think this means, "Stop doing all the work, *I am* the one who is *God*."**

How easily we forget that truth in the midst of all our running and doing. We are a high-tech, fix-it generation. We have learned how to resolve many complicated problems of generations past. So, why shouldn't we possess the knowledge to fix our lives?

Our lives are structured around a beehive of activity that begins the moment our feet hit the floor in the morning, and most of us like it that way. We have been taught from the time we were young to be productive and in control of our lives.

That ideal often carries over into our walk with the Lord. We get busy *doing* and ask God to *bless it*. Sometimes we can even be successful at it for a period of time. However, underneath we really are not resting and eventually the facade will begin to crack.

It can crack gradually through the wear and tear of daily life or radically through a crisis that invades our lives. For me, it was the impact of my physical illness. For you it may be the death or loss of a loved one, loss of a job, financial problems, etc. Crisis will always expose what is underneath. That is when we feel *out of control*.

None of us initially like feeling out of control, but when we can recognize which one of us is God and give Him the out-of-control circumstance, we can learn how to rest. I warn you, though, this action is a process. Our flesh and the patterns we have developed in the flesh resist change. It is usually only through repetition that we can achieve a true state of rest.

We are told in Scripture, "Therefore, make *every effort* to enter that rest" (Hebrews 4:11, NIV, emphasis mine). What rest is the author speaking of? Let's jump back a few verses, "There remains, then, a Sabbath-rest for the people of God; for anyone who enters God's rest also rests from his own work, just as God did from his" (Hebrews 4:9–10, NIV). Won't you strive to enter *His* rest?

Stop working…let God be God!

Rest in Me

This time is for a season,
The Savior seems to say.
Be at peace, My treasured one,
Come rest in Me this day.

Let My arms envelop you,
No fears come near your side.
Trust in Me for all your needs;
In My presence abide.

Don't you know that I know all
The secrets of your life?
Nothing can you hide from Me—
No worry, pain or strife.

Love, my child, I give to you,
To wipe your tears away.
Trust in Me, my treasured one
And do not feel dismay.

Hearing the Savior's Cry

I purposefully slipped into my secluded place of prayer—in a comfortable position that I have used the last several years in my practice of contemplative prayer. I am convinced that no one prayer posture is more holy than others. However, if we build a prayer closet—a place where we continually go to meet with our God—our minds and hearts can more readily travel there. We are in our humanness creatures of habit, so why not use that trait to bring us more easily into the presence of our Lord.

Nevertheless, as I lowered myself into my prone position on the floor, I recognized that this prayer hour would not come with ease. My heart was grieved over my past agonies and was stubbornly set on solutions to end the seemingly endless pain. I nervously adjusted the small pillow under my head and shifted my body around aimlessly to find a comfortable position. In actuality, it was my heart that was squirming to find a place of rest in its Savior.

In contemplative prayer it is important for the mind and heart to be fixed singly on the Lord. When I examined my mind I found it was racing in many different directions (none of them productive). And as I looked into my heart, the void I sensed was startling! I questioned myself and God, "Haven't we been over this ground before?" I was sick of reciting my story; wasn't Jesus also sick of hearing it? "After all, what could possibly be new about it?" I asked myself again.

In our practice of contemplative prayer, when our mind goes tripping off, we are to calmly notice what we are doing and gently bring our mind back to our simple acknowledgement of God's presence. In this instance, however, the misfortune that my flesh was paying attention to was greater than my desire to follow the Spirit, and my mind kept tripping. I tried to pay attention to my heart despite my desire to avoid the emptiness that I had sensed earlier. This seemed to be an easier task—only because it was a familiar place.

I finally managed to quiet my body and I sensed the Holy Spirit was quieting my soul. I did not want to rehearse my painful anecdotes before the Lord again, and so I decided to gather up all the pain attributed to those years and simply offer it to Him. There were no audible groans, although I became aware that my whole being was groaning inside. The Apostle Paul states it well:

> Now we know that if the earthly tent we live in is destroyed, we have a building from God, an eternal house in heaven, not built by human hands. Meanwhile we groan, longing to be clothed with our heavenly dwelling, because when we are clothed, we will not be found naked. For while we are in this tent, we groan and are burdened, because we do not wish to be unclothed but to be clothed with our heavenly dwelling, so that what is mortal may be swallowed up by life (2 Corinthians 5:1–4, NIV).

My inner groaning continued for a while, and as it progressed it increased in intensity. Inside my internal agony, I wondered where this was going when I saw in front of me a cross and my Savior draped on it. I noticed when my agony increased, His did also. Then I realized that His cries were becoming greater as mine were diminishing and I experienced a transfer of pain from me to Him. In a surprising interlude He screamed, "It is finished!"

His screams echoed through the hidden chambers of my heart and out into my troubled body. I recognized in that moment that His pain is the *only* answer to my pain. I now possess a new story for my inner being to rehearse—the story of my Savior on the cross crying out to me, "It is finished!"

You, too, can have a new message to speak into your pain and into your discouraged heart: "It is finished!"

Come to the Cross

Come to the cross of Jesus;
Leave all your burdens there.
Lay down your pain and sorrows,
Your anguish and despair.

Cast aside your piety,
Your pride, your pompous air
For He will only listen
To those who humbly bare—

Hearts, opened wide before Him
And bowing down in prayer.
They're looking to the Father
And seeking mercy there.

Look on the cross of Jesus;
His love He will not spare
To give you in abundance,
Pour over you with care.

Though you be heavy laden
And weighted down with care,
Our God is ever faithful;
He'll always meet you there.

CHAPTER FOUR

A Stream of Worship

Most of us do not feel like worshipping the Lord when we are in pain or filled with sorrow, but thankfully, how we feel is not a condition for true worship. Worship is about who *He* is, not who I am. Though, we usually need to remind ourselves of that truth again and again.

Worship is a condition of the heart that is birthed from an attitude of gratitude and adoration. Sometimes it is quiet and sometimes it is loud, but it should always emanate out of a right heart. Webster defines gratitude as "thankfulness for favors or benefits received" and adoration as "great love or devotion."[2] Yes, we can worship God for all the gifts and graces He brings to us (gratitude), although I believe it is a higher form of worship to simply love Him for *who He is* (devotion).

During times of crisis our hearts can grow dry and we may find that the stream of spiritual worship that once flowed through our hearts effortlessly is no longer present. Be encouraged, however, because it is in these dry places that our heart's devotion is purified and cleansed. When we persist in adoring *Him* a transformation takes place that moves us into a higher plane of worship and a larger revelation of His greatness.

Furthermore, it is from this place of revealed truth that the highest form of worship can be expressed—awe. Webster defines awe as "a mixed feeling of reverence, fear and wonder."[3] The psalmist writes, "Let all the earth fear the Lord; let all the inhabitants of the world stand in awe of Him. For He spoke, and it was done; He commanded, and it stood fast" (Psalm 33:8–9). As you can see here the psalmist clearly is extolling worshipping the Lord in fear and awe, simply for who He is.

Will you follow me as we worship Him together? He is worthy!

Worship is All About Him

One Sunday morning I wrote in my journal: "Today is my day of worship and I longed to awaken with a song gladly bursting from my heart. But instead, I was rudely awakened by my physical pain—again!"

I had gone to bed the evening before, tired from a long work week and a low level of lingering physical pain. I had hoped that sleep would restore my body and that I would wake refreshed and eager for a new day to begin. That was not the case.

Not feeling much better than the night before, I half-heartedly set myself to get ready for church. In my desperation to wake up, I headed straight to the refrigerator only to find that my usual protein drink was missing from the shelf where I kept it.

At that juncture, I shot a quick internal question to myself, "Do you *really* want to go to church today?"

I did not deliberate for very long, however, because experience has taught me that when I feel poorly is *precisely* the time to go to church.

When I arrived at church, the congregation was already singing and I had to squeeze my way through the aisle to gain a seat and join in. After the first few songs I realized that I was just going through the motions and I decided to bring my awareness back to something that I have learned throughout my trials—*I can praise God in and through all my circumstances*. My praise is not based on how I feel physically, emotionally, spiritually or situationally. It is based on who God is. Period!

I felt a release in my spirit as I once again reminded myself of that truth. I don't have to conjure up a certain feeling to worship God. I can just be me, right where I am today (in pain and not feeling particularly spiritual), praising God for *who He is*.

Our last song of the morning, fitly timed by the Spirit, made it extremely easy for me to enter in—"How Great Thou Art"!

Thank You, Lord, for that reminder that it's not about me—it's all about You!

Will you worship God with me, just as you are today? He is waiting there...

A New Song

Sing a new song to the Lord—
A new song to our King.
Let our voices now be raised,
An anthem let us sing.

He is worthy to be praised;
Bring glory to His name.
Enter the inheritance
The saints gladly proclaim.

Sing a song unto the Lord
Angels stop to listen.
Theirs is not the song to sing,
Which makes our hearts glisten.

Salvation! Sing to His name
Redemption shall be known
For those robed in righteousness
Rejoice before His throne.

Who, they ask, are those who stand
Dressed in their garments white?
They're the ones who overcame
The perils of the night.

> They come to tell their story.
> Do listen as they sing.
> They're singing now a new song,
> A new song to their King!

The Stream of His Forgiveness

The greatest gift we can receive from our Lord Jesus is the gift of forgiveness. He purchased it at the cross and it is a free gift to all those who will ask. Salvation is a one-time gift. We acknowledge to Him our need of a Savior, give Him our sin, and instantly He receives us into His family. Christ *is* our righteousness.

Paul writes to the Ephesians, "But because of His great love for us, God, who is rich in mercy, made us alive with Christ even when we were dead in transgressions—it is by grace you have been saved" (Ephesians 2:4 & 5, NIV). To the Romans Paul writes, "This righteousness from God comes through faith in Jesus Christ to all who believe. There is no difference, for all have sinned and fall short of the glory of God, and are justified freely by his grace through the redemption that came by Christ Jesus" (Romans 3:22–24, NIV).

The second grace gift of the cross is the healing and sanctification Christ continues to bring into our lives daily as we yield ourselves to Him. This is an ongoing process. If you have never given your life to the Lord and you seek healing—first surrender your life to Him. Once you have done that, the Holy Spirit (who lives in us after we experience salvation), will continue to reveal to you areas that still need the redemptive work of the cross to flow into you. Scripture tells us, "Therefore, I urge you, brothers, in view of God's mercy, to offer your bodies as living sacrifices, holy and pleasing to God—which is your spiritual worship. Do not conform any longer to the pattern of this world, but be transformed by the renewing of your mind" (Romans 12:1–2, NIV).

That was my prayerful cry one day when I knelt quietly on my living room floor. No one was home at the time. I removed the phone from its receiver and set the intention of my heart to seek God's holiness. Our Lord loves to answer that kind of prayer when we ask for His forgiveness and accept His cleansing, transforming holiness. Holy is who He is, and holiness is the transforming work He longs to do in each of our hearts. As I knelt there, I felt drawn by the Spirit into His *longing*.

This was my prayer. Can you make it yours?

A Sinner's Prayer

I came and knelt before Him,
My hands upheld my heart.
"Please cleanse me, my dear Savior,
Your righteousness impart.

"Forgive me—my dreadful sins
And of the stains which lie
Deep within this blackened heart
So deep within," said I.

There, the Spirit prayed for me
As I gazed at the sight.
God's blood dripped down on my heart,
Scarlet sins were turned white.

How awesome was the vision
I could not bear to move.
God's Spirit held me to Him,
His love, I felt Him prove.

"My God, I am not worthy
For You to come to me,
And cleanse this worthless being
From sin and set me free."

But then, I heard behind me
A voice so softly say,
"Peace, be still, My daughter for
I've washed your sins away."

The Eyes of Our Heart

Spring is that magical season of the year where buds of all sorts begin popping through the ground, adding color to our world and reminding us that *life* is present.

A thoroughly enjoyable and engaging time of day for me is when I escape to my deck that overlooks my favorite attraction in the yard—the lavish fishpond and waterfall. My attention is inevitably drawn to the center of the pond where water lilies are literally bubbling up creating a glorious mountain of greenery topped with bursting yellow blossoms cascading toward the sun.

One week I was forced to enjoy my garden in the early evening because it had been too hot to go outside during the day. I noticed something about the lily blossoms—they close in the evening! I am aware that many flowers do this, but I hadn't recognized it of my lilies. For several days I paid special attention to them in the daylight as well as evening, and confirmed my deduction—these lilies open to the sun and close when the sun goes down.

Our hearts are like that flower. When we look toward the *Son* and He is shining down on us, the eyes of our heart open and we flourish. As we remove our heavenward glances, our hearts close. It is easy to turn away from Him when we are experiencing trials. The darkness is very inviting. But, if our hearts follow the darkness, they will soon shut and the *life* that we enjoy in the Spirit will wither.

Signs of life appear as we worship. Worship looks like the lily blossom in the sun—petals opened wide, drinking in the warmth and fully inviting it in. Having received the sun, it opens even further and a dance begins between the Creator and His created—both enjoying the giving and receiving of life.

Will you look to the *Son* today and let Him open the eyes of your heart?

Through the Eyes of My Spirit

Little child so soft and meek,
On my knees—it's You I seek.
I humbly worship at Your feet,
Christ, the babe, I come and greet.

But, there is more my heart longs for;
His deity I bow before.
God incarnate—came to be
A sacrificial lamb for me.

My heart is stilled; my soul bends low.
I whisper, "God, how can I know
Your love that is greater than what I see?
These eyes can't envision eternity."

But there, in the moment, He came to speak,
"I know your frailty, but I am not weak.
My life is the candle to light your way;
I do not hide in the shadows this day.

"The eyes of My Spirit uncover My face.
Through the eyes of My Spirit you will see My grace.
My life I unfold before you today
As you come before Me to worship and pray!"

Stream of Grace

Our Savior not only promises to join us as we worship, He also promises to transform us. We cannot stay the same after spending time in the presence of God! The lily blossom opens in the light of the sun and reflects the beauty of its Creator, but it is not changed. We, however, are transformed by the *Son's* presence—changed *into* the very image of our Creator.

Come into the *Son's* presence and let Him grow you in His image!

Growing In Grace

How soft and gentle is the rose.
So lovingly the flower grows.
Created by the Master's hand
To spread His beauty o'er the land.

It reaches out for all to see.
Its splendor opened wide for me.
Bright petals soft about her face
Reveal the truth that's in God's *grace*.

How silently the Spirit sows
To make the ever graceful rose.
He works by *night* and never sleeps,
For in His hand the rose He keeps.

His love pours out upon this rose.
It changes as it grows and grows.
And then one day the rose will be
Transformed by Him for all to see.

Lord, as I sit and look to Thee
Make *me* a gentle rose to be
Growing in Your love and Your grace,
So all the world may see *Your* face.

CHAPTER FIVE

River of Love

I was thinking today about the love of God and the different ways He repeatedly demonstrates that love to us. Many times we fail to recognize His love. Often our eyes are blinded to His hand reaching out to us, or our hearts are turned from the warmth of His embrace.

Love means different things to every one of us. Usually, our perception of love is based on how we have *experienced* love in this lifetime and in particular our childhood. Often how we view our heavenly Father and His love is shaped by the way our parents loved us. It is true that healthy relationships later in life can correct some of our earlier misperceptions of God if parental love has been less than perfect. But our *expectations* of the Father's love that have been shaped by our past often limit our *experience* (the receiving) of His love.

One of the ways we can alter our response to God's love is through *spiritual understanding*. This is Paul's prayer to the church at Ephesus, and it is my prayer for you:

> "That the God of our Lord Jesus Christ, the Father of glory, may give to you the *spirit of wisdom and revelation to the knowledge of Him, the eyes of your understanding being enlightened*; that you may know

what is the hope of His calling, what are the riches of the glory of His inheritance in the saints..." (Ephesians 1:17–18, emphasis mine).

God's love for us is all about Him calling us. It is about His pursuit of us—*His* relentless, untiring, unwavering, sacrificial love.

God's Deliberate Pursuit of Me

I cannot remember the date or the title of the pastor's message, but I vividly remember that he spoke directly into my spirit and soul. His words captivated my heart and stirred it awake from a long deep sleep. In some ways it was as though I was hearing those words for the first time in my life as this slightly built priest leaned over the pulpit and with magnetic force bellowed out, "Abba, your Father, has an extravagant love for you."

He measured out that phrase several more times with equal magnetism and I soon realized that the only thing my senses were attuned to was the pastor, Abba Father, and me. Time held no relevance; neither did the faces around me, nor the knowledge that chapel would soon be over and I would have to return to class. The only notable occurrence was that which was happening inside my own body, spirit and soul. Years of pain had programmed my heart not to feel, and now it was responding to the beckoning of the Spirit's call.

The breaking open of my heart was sweet. Abba (the Hebrew word for "Daddy") was befriending the heart that had turned from Him for so many years. It was my misperception that He had deserted me through my physical trials (like my childhood abandonment by my dad and grandma), when in reality, it was my heart that had grown inattentive. I paused in that holy moment and noticed that my heart was now turned toward Him—stilled by such an amazing extravagant love.

Will you turn your heart toward the Father today? His greatest gift came in the person of Jesus Christ who sacrificed His life for you. That is an extravagant love!

The Light of His Love

Jesus, light of the world,
Do we see or care?
How can we realize
Your Spirit dwells there?

Shine into the darkness.
Uncover our eyes.
Expose our distortions
And our blackened lies.

His light comes to greet us,
It touches our hearts.
God's own infinite love
To us He imparts.

But, how can we fathom
God's wonderful grace
To reach out and touch us
When we've turned our face?

His Bride

Isn't it amazing that we are called "the bride of Christ?" It is not just a nice flowery thing for God to say. The picture that He desires us to grasp is a picture of deep intimacy.

Before the sacrifice of Jesus Christ, only the priests were allowed behind the veil in the Holy of Holies. However, Scripture tells us that at the death of Christ the temple veil was ripped apart (see Matthew 27:51), opening the way for *each one of us* who names Jesus as Lord to enter into the secret place. He personally invites us behind the veil.

Nevertheless, it is our choice whether to enter in or not. We may have to pull back *our veils* of protection, withdrawal or blame. This is sometimes difficult and leaves us feeling vulnerable. The reward, however, is great—a transparent love relationship with the One who is our greatest admirer.

Will you pull back the veil and allow Him in?

His invitation…

The Gift of My Love

Come My sweet one, My bride. Come behind the
veil where I invite you to dwell in My presence.
Do not stand afar off while My Spirit beckons
you to draw close. I long to know you
and the warmth of your embrace, the touch
of your hands holding Mine.

My desire is toward you—for you to know My
unending love for you. You are the treasure of My
heart and I have set My affection upon you.
You are the joy of My life; you fill My mouth with
laughter. Come My bride, play and laugh with Me.
Let Me fill you with My happiness.

This is My greatest goal and My delight. I long to
lift you up to where I am—where you will stand
forever by My side. My love for you is complete.
It lacks in no way. It can never fail.

Receive of My constant love for you this day.
Drink deeply from the rivers of love I have placed
in your heart and know that I, your Lover
and your Bridegroom, am with you.
Love, Jesus

A Wedding Vow

Tattered and torn
Damaged and worn
God give me grace
Reveal my place.

You see mighty.
I see frailty.
You seek embrace.
I see disgrace.

Eyes deceive me.
When will I see?
Why would You say,
"I'm yours to stay?"

Where is my sin?
You say, "Come in,
Enter my heart,
To never part."

I stand beside
This Lover's side.
Lord, bid me come
And I will come.

I open now,
Repeat His vow,
"Faithful and True,
I yield to You."

This was my response to my groom. He's waiting for yours!

Meditations from the River

Deeper, Deeper Still

One day the Lord spoke a phrase to me: "deeper and higher." He said, "The more that you invite Me into the deep places in your heart, the higher you will rise in Me." His Word states, "And He raised us up together with Him and made us sit down together [giving us joint seating with Him] in the heavenly sphere [by virtue of our being] in Christ Jesus (the Messiah, the Anointed One)" (Ephesians 2:6, AMPLIFIED).

How we love the high places! When we're sitting on the mountain top with Jesus, we enjoy the shared intimacy with Him, with our Father and His precious Holy Spirit. We love to rehearse His truths, share the knowledge of the kingdom, and exercise the authority given to us in that place. But, what about the deep places? What transpires between God and us in those places?

It is important for us to understand first of all that "nothing changes positionally." What do I mean by that? No matter whether we are young or mature in God, nothing we do or "grow into" will change our position (our standing) with Him. When we welcome Christ into our lives, we are *at that moment* catapulted into our heavenly status. We are *in Him* and everything of the kingdom that belongs to Him belongs to us at that time. Nonetheless, Christ calls us *into the deep* so that our knowledge and experience of Him will *deepen.* He delights in uncovering the depth of our fallen nature so that He can inhabit it and fill those places with the depth of His love.

The scripture that has depicted my heart's cry throughout most of my Christian walk is Ephesians 3:19. As I substitute "I and myself" for "you and yourself" in the Amplified version, will you read it as a petition from your heart as well?

> [That I may really come] to know [practically, through experience for myself] the love of Christ, which far surpasses mere knowledge [without experience]; that I may be filled [through all my being] unto all the fullness of God [may have the richest measure of the divine Presence, and become a

body wholly filled and flooded with God Himself]!
(Adapted from the Amplified Bible).

He invites each one of you…
"Come with Me and I will take you deeper."

Come With Me, Child

Come, My child
Into the depths of My love.
Will it hurt?
I asked of Him.
Sometimes, He said.
But, do you want to know Me?

Oh, yes, yes, I replied.
Come, take me to places
Even I have not seen.

But, I have seen them, He said.
And, they are not ugly to Me
Or shameful.
They are the jewels that will
Open the doors to My love.

But, Jesus, that doesn't make sense,
I told Him.
Those dark places seem *so* dark.

Child, dark is really light
Through My eyes.
Will you see what I see?
Will you hold the lantern of My Spirit
And walk down with Me into the hidden places?

I will, My Lord.
But, I need You to show me the way
And give me courage.
I will not fear if You are with me.

Yes, My child, yes
I will be with you.
But, will you choose to come?
I am calling to you.
Come to Me, come deeper, deeper still.

In the deep places His love will find you! Will you answer, "Yes, Lord I will come"?

Healing Waters

Within the many varied ways that the love of God has flowed to me, finding healing in His waters has certainly been one of them. Jesus *is* a God of healing. Even when we cannot see the evidence of that healing in our immediate experience, He is still at work moving us to the place of wholeness and completion in Him. Jesus purchased not only our salvation at the cross, but also our healing. Why wouldn't He then be committed to seeing that healing perfected in our lives? Here is an account from Scripture:

> When evening had come, they brought to Him many who were demon-possessed. And He cast out the spirits with a word, and healed all who were sick, that it might be fulfilled which was spoken by Isaiah the prophet, saying: "He Himself took our infirmities and bore our sicknesses" (Matthew 8:16–17; see also Isaiah 53:4).

Jesus diligently extended healing to all those who were sick when He walked this earth, and He is the same God today. Matthew 14:14

reads, "And when Jesus went out He saw a great multitude; and He was moved with compassion for them, and healed their sick."

As I have explained to you throughout these writings, Jesus did not come to me with the miraculous physical healing that I had imagined or desired (although that has not hindered me from pursuing healing and receiving from Him all the healing graces He has given along the way). Let me describe to you an experience when Jesus' healing flowed to me at a point of my greatest despair and transformed it into a place of my greatest hope.

Directed by the Spirit, I traveled across a continent to attend a conference where I heard that the Spirit of God was moving in some miraculous ways. As I boarded the plane leaving Los Angeles, my desperation was beginning to turn to expectancy. The Lord had, by this time in my life, healed my soul in various ways, although there lingered a deep and debilitating depression and severe spiritual dryness. I found that I was, once again, cycling back into the despair.

What I noticed about this cycle, however, was that my heart was positioned to search for the Lord. I felt more available to Him than I had at previous times and I whispered a grateful "thank you" to the Lord for that change. Still, I desired more healing and I made those intentions known to Him as well.

When I walked through the door of the meeting hall the first night, my heart was stirred. Excitement mingled with expectancy as I watched the exuberance of the worshippers. My heart was quickly drawn into this heavenly worship and I was amazed by the joy I felt invading me from within. I was pleased that my heart responded so eagerly to the Spirit's prompting. The worship lasted for over one hour (the longest I had ever experienced), but I could easily have continued worshipping.

The finale to that evening meeting was a prayer session—unique to me because of its "carpet time" (I later came to recognize this as "soaking prayer"). What was wondrous to me was the relaxed atmosphere and the emphasis that was placed on giving the Holy Spirit plenty of time and liberty to move as He wished. I was lying on the carpet enjoying the way the wind of the Spirit seemed to be flowing like waves over my body, when I envisioned myself lying in the river that flows from the throne of God.

Wave after wave washed over me as the Spirit brought this vision of God's throne room to life, restoring life to my darkened heart. After a while, I noticed that the waves, which flowed *over* me, were also flowing *through* me. I remained transfixed while a warm inviting liquid love penetrated every part of my body, soul and spirit; in return, every part of me echoed a prayer that was spoken from the pulpit, "More, Lord, I want more of You. I won't be happy until I have more."

The greatest thing about the liquid love of the Lord that day is that it healed my depression, spiritual dryness and it opened my spiritual eyes to a greater revelation and knowledge of His love.

Will you open your heart today to the liquid love of the Spirit? He wants to fill you.

Worship the Three In One

Lord, I come before Thee
To worship at Thy tent.
How I thank Thee, Father,
For riches to me sent.

No one but Thine alone
Is worthy of my praise.
Lifting my heart to Thee,
To Thee my voice I raise.

Christ the Lord is coming
As King for all to see,
Worshipping forever
The Son who died for me.

Glory to the Spirit;
I'm filled with His great love.
Flood me with Your presence,
Visit me from above.

> How I bless Thee, Spirit,
> The Father and the Son.
> Bowing my heart to Thee,
> I praise Thee, Three in One.

The Spirit delights in your coming!

CHAPTER SIX

Streams of Transformation

I remember the day I asked Jesus Christ into my heart as my Savior. A traveling evangelist was speaking at a nearby church I was attending. My heart pounded through most of the service and I was eager to respond to the altar call when he invited people forward to receive Christ. I was water baptized shortly after that day, and I thought that was it!

I soon realized that God had so much more for me—as He does for you! Not only does He desire that you grow in your relationship and knowledge of Him, He desires to transform you into His very likeness. In order to receive all God had planned for me, I became acquainted with prayers like, "More of You, Lord, less of me, more of Your Spirit. Your ways, not mine, Lord." Jesus was very eager to answer those prayers.

At the cross I found an answer for my every need. Most of all I found that the river that flows from His cross is a river of transformation that involves complete ownership by my Lord. My prayer, *"Let me be in You, God, and You in me"* has become central to this present season of my life.

Seeking more of God and desiring less of ourselves is the only way true change can take place in our lives. Oh yes, we can struggle to do it under our own power, but most of the deep change that needs to happen in our hearts can only come through the Spirit of God.

Having begun in the Spirit, why would we want to complete the work in the flesh? The Apostle Paul writes, "Are you so foolish? After beginning with the Spirit, are you now trying to attain your goal by human effort?" (Galatians 3:3, NIV).

Will you join with me and yield to the transforming power of the Holy Spirit?

My Night Terrors

Early in my Christian walk I would wake at night with fear gripping my soul. I didn't recognize what the fear was about; I just knew that I was filled with fear. *Terror* would actually be a better word because it was the kind of feeling that would grip my heart, shake me from my sleep and leave me motionless for hours, afraid to even whisper a prayer. I gradually learned how to battle my invisible foe by speaking the name of Jesus in my mind and forcing myself to get up and move into the living room. I had a plaque on the sofa table that contained the twenty-third psalm, and when I finally would be able to speak, I would read it aloud over and over. My ritual would continue for hours at a single setting and this practice extended over a period of several months.

Throughout this season of time the Holy Spirit began to illuminate the places in my soul that He desired to cleanse, and He gradually set me free from the bondage of my past. It was the baggage I was carrying that was kicking up all the fear. The enemy had owned me for many years, but now Jesus wanted to be my Lord. Every stronghold of the enemy had to be pulled down. Jesus desired to replace the fear with His love, and for this to happen I had to open my heart to Him in yet a deeper dimension. I had already received Jesus as my Savior, but there were areas of my heart that were still ruled by my flesh and the enemy. He wanted to be Lord of *all* that dwelled in my heart and being.

This was my prayer…

Unlock the Door

Unlock the secret doors of my heart.
Please, let all fear from me depart.
Where I have not dared to let You in,
Open the door and step within.

Do not let me hide from You in fear—
Locked within, unable to hear.
Give unto me the power and grace
To overcome, to see Your face.

Help me to know Your mercy and care
And Your love as *it* enters there.
Your love that is perfect, kind and true,
Love to fight the fear I've been through.

How can I measure Your matchless grace
Love—when I look into Your face?
How can I measure Your love for me
Unless I say, "Set my heart free."

Jesus wants to set your heart free, too!

The Lord's House

 The Lord spoke to me recently about houses. He asked me, "Whose house are you building? Is it yours, Mine or the enemy's?" Next, He began to elaborate what kind of building material each dwelling required.
 The prison-house of my past was where the enemy of my soul held me captive to sin, sickness and shame, but what about my present house?

Jesus showed me that every time I hide behind the prison doors of worry, fear or guilt, I am building the house of the enemy.

All that was required for my deliverance in the past is the same for today—an open door and an invitation to the Savior to come in.

Whose house are you building? The wounds of yesterday become the enemy's building blocks for your prison-house today.

The Prisons of Your Soul

We stand locked behind those prison doors
Confined within the prison of our *own* soul
Troubled by the present
Surrounded with the guilt, the failure, the
Fear of tomorrow, the pain of yesterday.

What will tomorrow bring?
Will it only bring more of the yesterdays?
Will it be the same as today?
Who will set us free?
Who is it that will pardon us?

His name is Jesus—Jesus!

The One who came to give us pardon
The One who came to set us free
He took *our* place before our Maker
He bore *our* sin
And in our stead, He died.

What more could we ask
He paid the price
He laid down *His* life
He set us free.

Meditations from the River

Season of Growth

The years of barrenness and coldness are a stark contrast to the years of fruitfulness—walking with the Lord, tasting of His goodness, seeing the fruit of His life manifested in our lives. The Lord is showing me that seasons of our lives follow the seasonal patterns of nature. Barrenness of soul that follows a season of fruitfulness is like the winter that follows fall.

Fall is the most colorful season of the year. The trees are brilliant with color and vibrant with life. You can almost hear a trumpet sound as you behold the dazzling countryside. What a contrast to winter! The trees are barren, naked and stripped of their vibrancy. Gone is the shout heralded by nature—replaced by a still quiet repose. The trees stand awkwardly against the gray skyline, motionless against the chilling wind.

This illustration from nature expresses the journey, or rapid descent of my soul from a place of exhilaration and anticipation to a place of stark existence. It is an unsettling experience, and yet it provides a wonderful opportunity for growth.

I asked God for a miracle. He said He's making *me* a miracle.

My Heart Sings

Can my heart be taught to sing
A new song unto Thee?
Can my spirit soar to heights
Unknown to man and me?

Can I see above the clouds
Where You are seated there?
Can I obtain the vision
To view the saints in prayer?

Can I rise above with Thee
And in Thy wisdom see
All the plans that You have held
Unfolding now to me?

Can I see amid the trials
Thy mercy and Thy care?
Can I see amid the trials
Thy hand extended there?

It would help so very much
If I could only see
The hand of my Beloved
Extended now to me.

A Life-changing Stream

There is a cozy little niche in my bedroom where I love to run to at night and meet with God. However, as much as I liked to meet Him there, I didn't go to that place very often. This was my nightly pattern: finish work about 9:30 p.m., drive home by 10 p.m., vegetate in front of the TV for an hour and fall into bed. I was anxious and exhausted most of the time, agitated by any intrusion by others on my time (especially family members), frustrated that I didn't have enough time or energy for my demanding schedule as a therapist, and generally felt out of sorts and out of control. I still felt connected to God, although I lacked the deep abiding peace that I once experienced and I didn't know how to change it. When I exerted some effort I could change my outer experience for a while, but it did not bring about the lasting heart change that I was longing for. I called out to God for help.

The Lord led me to refocus on what is labeled by some churches as *soaking prayer*. In past church ages we may have called it contemplative prayer, meditation or tarrying with God. I was already familiar with this type of prayer as I had engaged in it and been blessed by it many times at one particular retreat place that I attend. But now God was saying, "I want you to bring it home. It's not enough to go to where my river is flowing, jump in, get refreshed and leave. You need to *experience* the fresh flow of my Spirit every day." He instructed me to spend one to two hours a day just *soaking* in His presence—coming to Him with no other agenda except to spend time with Him. Naturally, when I heard that my head raced to, "But God, I have so little time as it is, where will I fit another thing in?" Then God was silent.

I'm sure many of you have experienced God's silences. Often what He is saying through that is, "OK, I have spoken and now it's up to you to evaluate your response." He wasn't saying, "I want you to give up your nightly TV." However, realistically that was the only free time I had. I entered into some dialog with God over giving up my only time to *myself*, but at the same time I was desperate to get *out of myself*—out of my old patterns and my old way of thinking and behaving—desperate enough to jump into the stream of His Spirit He was preparing for me in the evenings.

In that stream God *is* **recovering** me. I say "is" because the restorative process of soaking in His Spirit is just that—an ongoing process. The more we soak in God's presence, the more like Him we become. The dictionary meaning of "recover" is: "to get back (something lost, etc.), to regain health, balance or control."[4] I certainly needed to regain control! I was surprised that "regaining control" was part of the meaning. So, what I am experiencing is God recovering me back to the whole, healthy person I was intended to be. And, in the process, the Holy Spirit is helping me to regain a healthy sense of control and balance in my life.

In His stream His Spirit is also **uncovering** me—not in an unhealthy or a violating way—but in a loving and caring way. You can be sure that there is *safety* in the healing waters of God. Sometimes (especially if you have been violated in the past), it may be initially difficult to trust exposure to His Spirit, but as you do (even a little at a time), you will find He is full of grace. As I spend time soaking in His presence the impurities in my heart just naturally begin to float to the surface. He is continually cleansing and adjusting the attitudes that have led to my unwarranted behavior.

Most importantly, when we soak in the stream of His presence, we are in the process of **discovering** Him—Jesus Christ! Jesus is so willing—

no, more than that—He is *eager* to share more of Himself, more of His love, more of who He is with us every day. The fresh revelations I have gained recently of His personhood—His faithfulness toward me, His strength that is with me each day for every task, His ability to order my days—all have brought me such great peace! Each day I am more and more excited to find my quiet place at the edge of His stream and find Him waiting for me there.

He is waiting for you, too!

Drink Ye

Come, My child and drink of Me.
Fill your cup anew.
Come, My child and taste of Me.
Life shall come to you.

Drink ye and be satisfied.
Drink ye and be full.
Mine's the cup, which satisfies.
I *can* make you full!

Living water flowing out,
Flowing from My side.
Take and drink ye all of it,
In Me you'll abide.

All I Am I give to thee.
Enter now with Me
To My stream of sacrifice
Given out to thee.

The Father Always Makes Exchanges

One time my husband, Tony, attempted to return a purchase he made several years prior. As I had anticipated, the store refused to take it back. That interaction caused me to question, "What kind of merchant does the Lord resemble?"

I realized that the Lord is like a merchant who always accepts our misguided purchases. He never rejects the unused portions of our lives. And He is so generous that He repeatedly gives us *credit* out of His abundant storehouse in return. What a deal! He even exchanges the used and abused belongings in our soul for His bright and shiny gifts.

Can you imagine what a store with those practices would look like? I can. The trail of shoppers would be miles long. Why aren't there lines at the storehouse of God?

Take a look at Joseph's brothers (see Genesis 37–45). Their intentions and actions were all wrong. They sold Joseph into slavery and lied to their father that he was dead. Joseph later spent many years in prison unjustly. And, what does God do? He pours out multiplied blessings upon the brothers and saves the family from the famine in the land. God's ways are certainly not our own.

What do you want to bring God, today, to exchange?

My Tattered Gift

Lord, what do I have to bring You—
My brokenness and shame?
It does not seem a fitting gift
Amidst my guilt and blame.

I know You say to come to You,
Bring all with open hands.
You are a God of graciousness—
A God who understands.

But, when I survey my contents,
I shrink back in dismay.
How can this God of righteousness
Love this marred piece of clay?

There are cracks and hardened places
I labored to make new
With a glazed and shiny surface
To hide my hurt from view.

I labored long and hard, You know,
To keep those worlds apart.
But, the glaze could not hide from You
The pain deep in my heart.

I am weary of my journey
I long for something more.
Can I exchange Your righteousness
For the garment I wore?

I know it is a lot to ask
A God who sacrificed.
Your gift is a generous one
A gift that's highly priced.

But, now I dare to come to You,
My brokenness in hand,
To give to You my tattered gift
In exchange for one that's grand!

The Master Craftsman

Have you ever had the opportunity to observe a glass blower at work? I did, one summer afternoon while wandering through the gift and specialty stores at Knott's Berry Farm. My children and grandchildren desired a more energetic activity, but I stood in front of a glass craftsman mesmerized by the sight of colorful liquid glass being transformed before me.

I watched closely as the artist breathed into a long tube that held a glob of shimmering substance, and quickly out popped a bubble! After several minutes of twisting and turning the bubbled shape over a flame while blowing at various intensities, the crafter's able hands guided his tools to form the finished product. The shape, now recognizable, was a little dog, and its creator held it up to the glass window so that I could admire it with him. I smiled. It was fun to share that moment with a creator.

I continued to give my attention to the master craftsman as he created many different kinds of figures: dogs, cats, horses, clowns and ballerinas. I marveled at the way he skillfully turned his hands this way and that and blew with just the right amount of air at the right time to produce subtle changes in the glass. He never hesitated for a moment. He knew exactly what to do to fashion each piece according to his design.

Do not fear…the hands of the Master Craftsman are fashioning you. And, He knows exactly what He's doing!

The Potter's Hand

The clay is to the potter
What I am to You,
Yielding to Your gentle touch,
Yielding unto You.

Bending to Your perfect will,
Covered by Your grace.
How can I, this clump of clay
See You face to face?

Looking unto God above,
Looking unto Him,
Seeking for His perfect love,
Abiding within.

> He molds me with tender care.
> In His hands I rest.
> He makes me as the vessel
> That *He* believes best.

Streams of Glory

Shame is a powerful emotion that we wear like a sacred badge or hide in the internal recesses of our soul.

There are many sources and types of shame. Healthy shame tells us we have erred against the standards of God, of society, or our own, and it alerts us to our error so that we can rectify it. Unhealthy shame, on the other hand, is deadly to our soul and interferes with our sense of self and our relationship with God and others. Unhealthy shame is always antagonistic to our knowledge and acceptance of the love of God.

Unhealthy shame can impact us through abuse, neglect and abandonment, or it can be associated with prolonged poverty or ill health. Any lengthy trial has the potential of sickening our souls to the point where we feel the grave helplessness that leads to shame.

Unhealthy shame in any form produces the same results. When we are afflicted in our soul, we shrink from the glorious potential God has purposed for our lives. If I were to think of an antonym (opposite) for the word "shame", it would be *glory*. God's glory, filled with light and majesty, is such a contrast to the degenerating darkness that shame produces. However, it is *into* our degenerating darkness that God comes to deposit His glory.

> At our deepest darkest hours
> A still small light shall shine
> Reflecting not our image,
> But reflecting Thine.

This is the glory He deposited into my shameful state one day…

One day while I was in prayer, Jesus revealed to me a picture of a shiny silver goblet with delicately carved handles on either side. I thought to myself that it had the appearance of a winner's cup, a trophy, and the Lord said, "That's right, and this is you."

As I watched Him, He held me up and displayed me before all the hosts of heaven (particularly in the face of the enemy) as a winner—an overcomer. I questioned, "How can He label me as a winner?" I certainly did not *feel* like a winner.

Then I stood on tiptoe and peered over the lip of the cup, down into the deep chalice and what I saw was blood—His blood. My heart beat excitedly as I gave credence to His message, "I was an overcomer because of the blood of the Lamb that filled me, *His* vessel."

I watched as He, the Master-craftsman, continued to elevate me, the silver goblet, His masterpiece, before Himself when an image appeared on my surface. It was *His* image that was being reflected. I was amazed, although my amazement was drawn inward as I reflected on my internal state. "Where did my shame go?" I asked.

He whispered, "What shame? All I see is *My glory*!"

Will you let His glory transform your shame? He longs to make you a winner!

The Healing Flood

The blood of Jesus flows to me,
The blood that runs from Calvary.
How sweet the blood, how sweet the flood
Flowing from His side.

The blood of Jesus beckons me.
It pours out sacrificially.
His love so pure, His love so sure,
To cover and to comfort me.

My Jesus, Your dear flood I see
Flowing and enveloping me;
Love from Your side, come now abide
Within my soul—to set me free.

CHAPTER SEVEN

Streams of Service

Jesus gave the twelve disciples these instructions as He sent them out, "As you go, preach this message: 'The kingdom of heaven is near.' Heal the sick, raise the dead, cleanse those who have leprosy, drive out demons. *Freely you have received, freely give*" (Matthew 10:7–8, NIV, emphasis mine). This command of Christ was not just for those twelve followers, but it is part of His great commission to all believers (see Mark 16:17–18). I confirm that Jesus desires to pour into each one of us His healing, deliverance and added blessings just because He loves *us*.

In addition to receiving His blessings, we are to give out spiritual benefits and allow them to flow to others. We are Christ's ambassadors—His hands and feet on this planet we are journeying through.

It is important for us to remember that our sacrifice is only possible because of His sacrifice on the cross. It is His power and not ours, which is given to us through the Holy Spirit. We are to follow His plan and calling on our lives, not our own. Sometimes His path requires brokenness—a breaking off of the old ways to make room for the new. The trials of life not only refine us, but as we yield to the working of the Spirit, they can open us more fully to the move of the Spirit working *through* our lives to others.

Will you open your heart to the Holy Spirit? He desires to move in you and through you!

Love

Love, in the form of a dove
Coming from the Father.
Love, in hands extended out
Reaching one another.

Love, in the form of a man
Who came and died for me.
Love, with hands now lifted high
I give it back to Thee.

Streams of Sacrifice

It was an early summer day as I stood in my living room worshipping and singing praises to the Lord. My body felt warmed and oddly contented as the tepid air that streamed through the open window surrounded me. I was not aware that soon a different stream of air would embrace me—the breath of the Holy Spirit. As I stilled myself in my humble, commonplace sanctuary, all of my senses and attention were riveted on that precise moment in time; I became keenly aware that I would be perfectly content to remain there forever!

As I remained inside this capsule of time, I grew mystified by a wondrous, captivating presence that was seeping into my heart as it saturated the room. Vacillating between intense exuberant worship and stunned silences, I began to notice that this breath of God was swirling around me. The heavenly stream of His Spirit continued and the weight of His felt presence on my body increased until I could no longer stand. I lay prostrate before Him.

After awhile, I began to feel the weight of my sin and I started repenting before God. An image of the cross instantly appeared before me. The base of the cross was situated directly above the top of my head and as I strained to look up, I saw Jesus hanging there. I was overcome by my sin until He spoke to me, "My blood has covered *all* your sin." Amazed, I paused to drink deeply of this moment so I would not return to my guilt and shame.

Then the Lord made a request that took me a while to answer. He asked, "Are you willing to be broken and suffer for Me?" A scripture appeared in my mind: "That I may know Him and the power of His resurrection, and the *fellowship* of *His sufferings*, being *conformed to His death*, if, by any means, I may attain to the resurrection from the dead" (Philippians 3:10–11, emphasis mine).

Jesus made it clear that a yes or no response would be equally acceptable, although He also made it known that my response would alter some of the events in my life. He instructed me to think about my commitment before I answered. I recognized that my highest good would come through an affirmative response, but at the same time I was beginning to experience the gravity of my decision. The Holy Spirit remained forcefully present with me as I considered my action. I inquired within, "What exactly am I willing to yield to Him? What will this brokenness look like?"

As I lay there, I reviewed the last four weeks during which I had been engaged in an ongoing fast. The focus of my prayer and fasting had been that God would lead me into a deeper place of dedication to Him. In response, Jesus led me into a prayer session where I laid down my possessions, loved ones, career and ministry at His altar. I marveled at this loving God who had been tenderizing and preparing my heart all along.

God the Father's overarching goal is that we be conformed to the image of His Son. Anything that comes against that goal will have to be moved out of the way, even if that *something* is our plan for healing, prosperity or comfort. Jesus knew my answer already. With all my heart I desired that the *full* purpose of God be worked out in my life. I said, "Yes, Lord, I am willing."

What is the Holy Spirit asking of you today? Are there ways that He has been preparing your heart for the "highest good" He has for you?

Broken Bread, Poured Out Wine

Poured out wine
Broken bread
Do that, Lord
Through me

Take me
And use me
I give my life
To Thee

Give me now
That cup to drink
Which once You drank
For me

Break the bread
I give to Thee
Let it be broken
Now for Thee

Let me, Lord
Give back to Thee
The gift
You've given me

And let it be
A gift
You'll use
For all eternity

A Moment's Meeting

As I sit and reflect on the moments when God spoke to my heart, I am mindful that no single message impacted me more greatly than the one I am about to reveal to you. I assess it as powerful because it transformed my heart, prayer life and vision. The Word of God, when it comes to us, should not just excite us. Yes, it is exhilarating when God speaks, but that word is also carried along by the Spirit of God and with Him comes kingdom power to ignite and create something new in us or in our circumstances. His word should impregnate us with great expectation and incite us to action. That is what this word did for me:

The speaker, in a corporate prayer meeting I was attending, was praying that the Holy Spirit would anoint us for the task of intercession. He began to call out different focal points: missions, the unsaved, etc. Then he declared, "There are those of you who will minister to the abandoned."

Instantly, my spirit and soul were grieved and a picture appeared to me. It was a sea of broken children, infants and young children, all battered, forgotten and unloved. It was an image that overwhelmed my heart. There was no end to this *sea*. As far as I searched in every direction, the sea of bodies remained endless.

I began to weep from the depth of my being and cried out, "God, please heal the babies." As the vision continued I cried out again, "Oh, God, there are so many, so, so many." My soul was stunned and sickened by what I saw. I realized that the Spirit of God was imparting to me the very heart of God that was grieving for His lost and damaged children. Only by the Spirit of God could I continue to plead, "Lord, heal Your children."

The Lord reminded me through this vision of the ministry He has called me to: to heal the brokenhearted, the broken, the battered child inside every wounded adult. This vision was more than a word of confirmation, however. It strengthened my awareness that this calling not only *originates* in the heart of God, but it is He and His Spirit who will empower the *work* of the ministry. The focus then becomes, "What is in the heart and mind of God? What does He want to do?" and not "What is my calling?" or "What can I do for Him?"

In that moment a major shift occurred in my soul, stirring me to a different kind of action—an action to pray, to seek the heart of God and then to minister. For an extended season I had been praying, "Lord, anoint and send me to Your people. I hear Your call." His reply was, "First, I must give you *My* heart for them."

In intercession we receive, I am sure, only a measure of the sorrow that consumes Him, but it arrives with the impartation of His Spirit to break open the hidden chambers of our hearts and fill them with His compassion.

Seek compassion first, ministry second.

A New Heart

I lay my heart open to You;
I lay it on the altar.
Take it in Your hands, my Savior,
And shape it and change it,
Enlarge it.

Take the fear that lies within
And the hurts,
The callused and stony places.
Make them soft,
Pliable in Your hands.

Do with me what You will
For I am Yours.
You are the Lord that changes not.
Change me.

Mold me into Your image, Lord.
Change me into Your shape;
Make my will
Yours.

Meditations from the River

For I desire to be like *You*,
To walk Your way,
The path that You have laid
Before me.

My Savior,
Press Your life into mine.
Make me Yours.

Can you make this prayer yours? You will never regret it. His way is perfect!

Times and Seasons

The cool air brushed against my face as I positioned myself on my outdoor deck for my morning devotion. As I ingested the beauty of my garden, I was thankful that we had spent time, energy and money the previous spring on landscaping the back yard. Even though the rich foliage and brilliantly colored blossoms of spring were missing, it still was a wonderful and exhilarating sight. Winter in California is much unlike the blistery cold I had experienced in New York; nevertheless, the brisk air and dense clouds reminded me that winter had arrived.

As I sipped my coffee and set my heart to commune with God, I noticed one plant hanging close to where I sat. It was unique because it was one of the few plants adorning my patio that remained in bloom. The bright pink spray of color caught my attention, and I realized that the Lord was alerting me to its presence. I became aware that there was a *message* for me personified in this plant, and I whispered a simple prayer that God would convey to me His intention.

In the stillness of that moment His words were clear, "I will cause you to blossom in the *winter*." I acknowledged to myself that I had heard accurately, but I was unsure of its implication. The first interpretation that came to my mind the Lord discarded. So, I continued to sit in silence, rehearsing the word and waiting for further revelation.

Then, as gently as the soft breeze embracing my body, the Holy Spirit breathed into my soul, "You are in the *winter of your life*." He elaborated, "Your first twenty years were your spring years—a time of birth and new growth. Your second twenty years were your summer years—a time of fruitfulness in the knowledge of the Lord, but also a time of heat and testing. Your third twenty years were your fall years—a time of bareness (sickness and spiritual dryness) and a preparation for winter (school). Your forth twenty years will be a time of blossoming. Contrary to nature, I will cause you to bloom in winter." The writer of Ecclesiastes states, "To everything there is a season, a time for every purpose under heaven" (3:1).

What season of your life are you experiencing? It may be fruitful or dry, joyful or sorrowful, restful or laboring. You may be at the beginning of your life or at the end. You may have known the Lord one year or fifty years. What is God speaking to you about *this* season of your life? Our times and our seasons are in His hands and His plan is the only one that is perfect.

I really needed that word from God in this season of my life because I had a growing unsettledness that somehow I had missed the fulfillment of God's purpose for me. And yet, here He was, saying, "I know where I'm taking you. The best is yet to come. Keep going. Keep serving Me. You're right on track. This is *My* plan." That is great to know!

Your times and seasons are in His hands, too!

The Master Planner

> Sometimes we see our lives
> Like particles of sand.
> But, we're a lump of clay
> God fashions in His hand.
>
> He holds the form firmly
> With purpose and design.
> "I won't drop or harm you,
> For you see you are Mine."

He begins with a name,
Bob or Sally or Joe,
Then declares it out loud
For all beings to know.

"This being is special;
I have taken great care
To show you My image
That I willingly share.

"I open before you
My script for each lifetime.
I am sure of the plan
For it fits with *My* time.

"I created the earth
And fashioned each season.
Won't you trust in Me now
And not your own reason?"

You can trust the Master Planner...

Serving the Cross

The longer I journey with the Lord and am impacted by Him in my own life as well as those I serve, the more I recognize that the cross is our foundation! Our lives can become scattered inside and out, but Christ's sacrifice is the rock we can return to and stand upon.

His action extends for all time and is complete. He left nothing out, nothing undone. That is why we can trust it. Our actions are incomplete; only when they are linked to the cross do they have value.

As Christ hung on the cross, blood and water poured from His wounded side (see John 19:34). It is to this precious flow—the spilling forth of His love—that we can go and find the healing waters. *Our every need was taken to and absorbed by His cross.*

Serving Christ is an awesome privilege because when we serve Christ, we serve the cross.

He's Alive!

He is raised—Christ has risen!
The tomb lays open bare.
He is raised—Christ has risen!
His body is not there.

He died for you—died for me
And in the tomb He lay.
But death could never hold Him;
He rolled the stone away.

The guards feared and were shaken
And fell upon the ground;
Asleep they did not notice
God's *glory* did abound.

The presence of the Spirit,
Uncovering His light,
He's coming down from heaven
With power and with might.

The whisper of the angels,
So softly they did speak
To Mary while she wept there
Seeking the One so meek.

He has raised—they confided;
He's not stolen away.
He went into Galilee;
Go tell each one this day.

Tell them of the miracle,
Christ Jesus is alive!
It happened as is written.
Now, let your hearts revive.

So spoke the ancient prophets
The Scriptures now unfold;
God's plan through all the ages
Has not been left untold.

Jesus Christ, He has risen!
With the Father—the Son
And promises the Spirit
To each and every one

Who believe the angels' news
About Christ, God's own Son—
Who died and now lives again
The victory He's won!

Sin and death no longer rule;
Hell's strength will not survive.
The grave has been found empty,
The Savior—He's alive!

Life is our heritage! Won't you reach out today and receive?

The Lord has a destiny, a perfect plan, for you. The only requirement for its fulfillment is that you embrace it. Will you open your heart today to the One who can love your heart to health and pour through you to a sick and needy world? His river is flowing. It never stops. But, you are the only one who can determine how deep you will go.

Can you allow your heart to cry out with mine, "Yes, Lord, take me deeper still!"?

About the Author

Carol Romeo is a seasoned author, speaker, and marriage and family therapist. She has crafted five books throughout the past 2 decades of serving others with the accumulated wisdom that she gained throughout her personal recovery process and her experience counseling others. Carol received her bachelor's degree in psychology and her master's degree in marriage and family therapy from Azusa Pacific University. Carol feels passionate about her goal to bring wounded people to health and is convinced that it is vital to include spiritual training as part of the healing. This understanding moved her to gain a master's degree of practical ministry from Wagner Leadership Institute and functioned as a prayer counselor in numerous churches.

While thinking about how I want to present myself and my works to you, I was reminded by the Lord that the contents of my books are really a journey. First of all, they are **my** journey. Each book describes my struggles during that part of my life and how the Lord healed, delivered me and ushered me into a **new me**. This is a process whose stages are dictated by Christ and Him alone. It is a process designed for each of us individually because He alone knows our needs and what we need from Him to transform us into the **new whole** persons we were meant to be.

Books authored by Carol Romeo

Meditations from the River: Healing Waters for Troubled Times. Copyright 2008 by Carol Romeo. AuthorHouse Publishing, Bloomington, Indiana.

Traveling with the Life-Giver: A Spiritual Journey Through Recovery from Abuse. Copyright 2012 by Carol Romeo. AuthorHouse Publishing, Bloomington, Indiana.

Expect the Miraculous: A True Life Story of the Extraordinary Power of God. Copyright 2017 by Carol Romeo. WestBow Press, Bloomington, Indiana.

Be a Powerful Woman of God: A Testament of His Goodness. Copyright 2021 by Carol Romeo. Trilogy Christian Publishing, Tustin, California

Journey into Wholeness: Steps to Emotional Wholeness. Copyright 2022 by Carol Romeo. Brilliant Books, San Francisco, California

www.ingramcontent.com/pod-product-compliance
Lightning Source LLC
Chambersburg PA
CBHW060407080526
44583CB00012B/494